EVERYTHING I NEED TO KNOW, I LEARNED PLAYING PICKLEBALL

STORIES FROM THE COURT
LESSONS FROM THE SPORT

RICK BROIDA

Print ISBN: 979-8-89589-853-6
eBook ISBN: 979-8-89589-854-3

Printed in the United States of America.

First Edition

For Jim

Thanks for taking me to school

TABLE OF CONTENTS

Introduction — vii

Then — vii

Now — xi

Before — xiii

After — xv

Lesson 1: Try New Things — 1

Lesson 2: Say Hello — 5

Lesson 3: Stop Apologizing — 9

Lesson 4: Step Out of Your Comfort Zone — 13

Lesson 5: Don't Judge a Book… — 19

Lesson 6: Be Gracious — 25

Lesson 7: Don't Give Up — 27

Lesson 8: Forgive Your Mistakes — 31

Lesson 9: Be a Gentleman (or a Lady) — 39

Lesson 10: Don't Believe Everything You Read (Except This, Obviously) — 43

Lesson 11: Pivot! — 47

Lesson 12: Patience Really is a Virtue — 49

Lesson 13: You Win Some, Your Learn Some — 55

Last Lobs — 59

Epilogue — 63

Acknowledgements — 69

THEN

It's Sunday morning, circa 2010, and I'm lacing my shoes for a couple hours of basketball at the local gym. These are pickup games, full court, with teams randomly thrown together from a clipboard hanging on the gym wall. Write your name and wait your turn. After each game, the next group of five hits the court, while the team coming off makes a beeline back to the clipboard.

I'm in my late 30s, which should mean I've brought a couple decades' worth of hoops experience with me. It doesn't. I came to the game only a handful of years earlier; it just wasn't on my radar as a kid. Tennis was the family sport, so I missed out on those essential driveway years of layups and jump-shots and games of HORSE. We had no hoop, so I had no game.

But I'd fallen hard for basketball, and with a full-time job and two young kids at home, these weekend games were my best – my only – chance to play.

The gym is packed as always, a cacophony of shoes squeaking, balls bouncing, and players shouting – often angrily. At least three or four times per morning, a game would grind to a halt as someone challenged a foul or disputed an out-of-bounds. Tempers would flare, expletives would fly. This made me uncomfortable for reasons I didn't fully understand until years later. Thankfully, I never saw an actual fight break out — but a few times it came close.

It's competitive out there. Cutthroat. If your team wins, you get to stay on the court and keep playing. Losing means back to the bottom of the clipboard, which could mean sitting on the sidelines for another 10 or 20 minutes, depending on how many others are ahead of you. Nobody wants that.

And everyone's good, really good, like they've been playing since they were kids shooting layups and jump-shots in their driveways.

I am not good. I'm borderline bad. I don't trust my left hand with the ball, so I constantly dribble with my right; easy pickings for the defense. When someone else on my team brings the ball down court, I scramble around trying to get open, not really knowing where to position myself. (In one game an exasperated center stopped dribbling at the top of the key, looked me square in the eye, and yelled, "Stop moving!") On the rare occasion I get an open look at the basket, the shot invariably ends up a brick or air-ball.

It wasn't that I lacked athletic prowess. As a kid I was a decent little-league first-baseman and backyard Nerf-football player. Mostly I played tennis: camps, lessons, long summers on the court. I loved sports, and over the years I dabbled in racquetball, wallyball, and kickboxing. I liked to compete, liked to win as much as the next guy. I wasn't without coordination or stamina or zeal, but where basketball was concerned, I was without skill — and, therefore, confidence.

Not just game confidence, but social as well. Although I showed up nearly every weekend for months at a stretch, bonds were not established, friendships not forged. At most I might get a chin-up "Hey" of recognition from someone. I made meager attempts at conversation, but never knew what to say. It was like I'd joined a club that had only grudgingly accepted my membership; my seat was at the end of the table, everyone looking the other way. Nobody to pass the salt – or the ball.

At one point I thought I had a solid "in" with one of the guys. I'm Jewish, and there was one Sunday just after Rosh Hashanah, the Jewish new year. This guy, who I'd seen many times on the court, was clearly Jewish as well; I say "clearly" because, well, he looked it. I don't mean this in any way other than I have a well-honed Jew-dar; I know a fellow tribesman when I see him.

Anyway, in between games, I find myself standing next to this guy – let's call him Elijah; *that's* how Jewish he looked – and I said, "Hey, happy New Year." Because that's what you say during Rosh Hashanah.

Elijah looked at me like I'd just insulted his mother. "What do you mean?" he said, making no effort to disguise his annoyance.

"Uh, aren't you Jewish?"

"What makes you say that?"

I don't remember what word-vomit escaped my mouth next, but eventually he copped to it – yes, he was Jewish – and I tried to recover with related small talk. What temple did he attend?

But he wasn't having it. Apparently this guy didn't know he looked like an escapee from rabbinical school, or at least he didn't like being called on it. Either way, it was not the start of a beautiful friendship; he stormed off and I was left to wonder what was wrong with me.

That banner moment led to another one later the same morning: Coming off the court after a loss, I rushed to the clipboard, wrote my name, and handed the pencil to the next player. As I turned to go, I noticed that he looked at my name, did some quick math, then let someone else jump the line. The meaning was clear: He didn't want to be in the next group if it meant having me on his team. He'd rather *sit out longer*. I guess my lackluster skills were well-known by this point. Getting stuck with me meant a greater likelihood of losing.

This lack of acceptance, this borderline hostility, left me feeling exactly how you'd think it would: embarrassed, unwanted, hopeless. Coming onto the court each week in this headspace, well, it didn't help my game. Just call me Tragic Johnson.

Not that I didn't try. Efforts to improve my skills included installing (at long last) a driveway hoop so I could practice at home; signing up for an expensive weekend basketball camp for adults; and even reading how-to books – quite possibly the most useless tool for learning a sport. (Remember, this was pre-YouTube. If only I'd had access to the amazing video library available today, I'd be writing about basketball's life lessons.)

Mostly, though, I just showed up for these weekend games, played badly, then went home feeling miserable. Eventually I stopped showing up.

NOW

It's Friday morning, 2024. I'm lacing my shoes, limbering up. I'm a few towns over, where a neighborhood tennis court has been converted into two pickleball courts. The sun is shining; summer is in full swing. I've been invited for doubles with some guys I've met in leagues and drop-in games. I'm 55; the rest are around the same age or older. Some are retired, some (like me) are playing hooky before work. We're all good players, probably in the 4.0-4.5 range, though I do feel a bit of Imposter Syndrome watching the other four play their first game. Look how perfectly Rick F. hits his third-shot drops. Look at Jim's cannon of a forehand; he smacks the ball so hard you can hear it whistle through the air. And check out Ernie and Randy miraculously volleying back those bullets. What am I doing here? I can't compete with these guys. It's just a matter of time before someone volunteers to sit out rather than partner with me.

But that doesn't happen. I rotate in and the games are close, competitive. And I have so. Much. Freaking. Fun. There's laughter and good-natured ribbing and whoops of delight over impossible shots. Everyone wants to win because of course they do, but no one cares much if they lose. Even better, no one gets mad if I miss an easy dink or launch a ball past the baseline. These guys are like me: They want to get some exercise and have some fun. And there's nothing more fun than pickleball.

Nothing.

I'll die on this hill.

In the nearly three years since I started playing this game, I've met more new people than in the last 30 years. With rare exception, they're all upbeat and welcoming, infected by the same joyful spirit. Why? Pickleball is easy to learn, accessible to all ages, and uniquely social. And something about this Friday-morning gathering, this relaxed, laugh-filled experience, drove home a realization: These are my people, and this is my game.

BEFORE

It's a dark winter night in Pinckney, Michigan, and as I walk the long hallway leading to the Navigator School gymnasium, I can hear the telltale sound of shoes squeaking on polished floors. The thwock of a paddle striking a ball. Shouts and laughter and the jovial chatter of people engaged in sport.

I'm equipped with little more than mild curiosity and the cheapest gear I could find on Amazon. Walking beside me is Jim, my sister-in-law's significant other. Affable, barrel-chested, still hitting the gym daily at the age of 73, he'd been playing this game for over a decade, long before it was cool, long before anyone had heard of it.

"You should try it," he'd encouraged me a few times. But I couldn't muster much interest. With my tennis background, I found myself scoffing at the shrunken court, the plastic whiffle ball, the old people in knee braces. I was still taking kickboxing classes, for heaven's sake. This just sounded silly – especially the name.

This was November, 2021, right in the collective consciousness' transition period between "Pickleball? What's that?" and "Oh, pickleball, I've been meaning to try it."

More to the point, it was in the early days after the Pandemic, when the miracle of vaccines had finally freed us from confinement. The game itself didn't sound that great, but I was definitely ready for something, anything, that might get me out of the house and moving my body.

In the gym were four makeshift courts, all of them full, with maybe a dozen other players waiting to rotate in. Jim escorted me to an upper level, where a genial instructor who looked about 97 put me on another makeshift court and laid out the basics.

"This is the kitchen; you can't hit a ball in there unless it bounces first."

"After you serve, you have to let the return bounce; you can't hit it in the air."

"You're the second server, so the score is 3-4-2."

Um, what?

Yeah, pickleball scoring will wreck your brain. It's arguably the hardest thing to learn.

Because I'd played baseball and tennis as a kid and ping-pong my entire life, I had the basic hit-ball-with-thing skills in place. After some practice, I moved downstairs and nervously joined the rotation. I barely knew where to stand. I definitely couldn't wrap my head around scoring. But to my surprise, all the other players were patient and accommodating; they just seemed to be having fun and didn't mind helping a newcomer.

Weird.

After a few games I started to catch on, and even hit a couple good shots that revived some long-dormant endorphins. Oh, hey, sports. Long time, good to see you.

AFTER

It's a warm August morning, nearly two years after I first picked up a pickleball paddle, and I'm about to step onto a makeshift podium to pose for a photo. I'm still in disbelief; the hardware hanging from my neck isn't bronze or silver; it's gold. I'd just won a 3.5+ singles tournament. My first-ever singles tournament. My first solo victory in any sport. In any anything.

It. Felt. Amazing.

Sure, it was a small event at a local sports club — the same one where basketball had chewed me up and spit me out years earlier — just me and four or five other guys. But up till that point I'd mostly played doubles, which I'd say occupies 95% of pickleball. Singles was my thing back when I played tennis, and I'd never been great at it. My dad was the trophy-winner there. But that summer of 2023 I'd signed up for an almost laughable number of leagues and tournaments; I just wanted to play as much as possible. I'd long since become a card-carrying pickleball fanatic. Singles tournament? Why not?

And as I walked to the parking lot with my gold, I felt a lump in my throat. I wished my dad could have been there to see it; he'd passed away the year before. I know he'd have been proud. But I was so proud of my-self, too; somehow I'd beaten everyone else in the tournament, despite feeling certain they were better players. Hence a few happy tears.

To this day I cherish that victory. And the more I think about it, the more I realize how much this game with the silly name has taught me. In fact, I'm starting to think that everything I need to know – well, you've seen the cover.

What follows are the lessons pickleball has imparted and how I've tried to weave them into everyday life. I'll also introduce you to a few folks I've met along the way, because they're the ones who helped me learn those lessons. There have been a few crummy moments along the way, but, hey, that's life, right? And to borrow from *Ted Lasso*: Pickleball *is* life.

TRY NEW THINGS

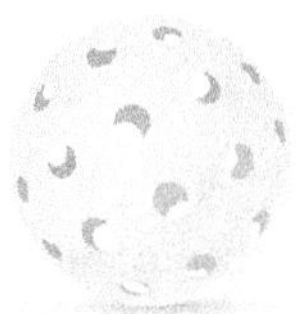

When was the last time you tried something completely new? Perhaps during the Pandemic, when so many of us struggled to find ways to occupy our lockdown time. Maybe you picked up the guitar or learned to knit. Maybe you started that novel you'd always been meaning to write or learned to perfect homemade bread.

Much of that was born from a need to stay sane during an insane time. But as a general rule, people tend to shy away from new things, especially as they get older.

You can probably guess why; it's all about the F-word.

"Fear is what drives our emotions," says life coach Ryan Burtanog, "and it can keep us from moving forward."

Guilty as charged. I can think of countless times I had the opportunity to try something new or different and said no – not even realizing, at the time, that I was letting fear dictate my decision.

On a small scale, Burtanog says, this can be something as basic as trying a new dish at a restaurant. When you order the same old thing, "you do that because it's familiar. You know exactly what you're going to get and it makes you happy. You feel safe."

If you do decide to be adventurous and order that new thing, there's always the chance you won't like it. And that just reinforces your fearful instinct; you might end up angry at the restaurant or, more likely, at yourself, he says.

As I mentioned in the introduction, I had very little interest in pickleball. But was I skeptical of the game itself, or did I fear failure? Did I think I'd go out there and play poorly and get mocked by others? End up feeling embarrassed like I did on the basketball court?

No doubt a combination of all those things. I'm lucky I had Jim to not only encourage me, but also accompany me during my first forays onto the court. Everything's easier if you have a friend by your side.

And like anything else, trying new things becomes easier the more you do it. "We might still have that fear," Ryan says, "but it's driven away by our excitement of the unknown positive consequences. We build resilience in our lives. We can start to believe in ourselves more."

Recently I watched a TikTok video in which a theater full of people sang along to Toto's "Africa." This was orchestrated (literally) by a tiny group called Pub Choir, which started in Australia but occasionally tours in the U.S. (Look it up. Seriously.)

Here's the thing: I don't sing — not in front of others, anyway. I'll belt out Billy Joel's "We Didn't Start the Fire" when I'm in the car, by myself, but if you want me to sing in a group setting, you'd better be brandishing some kind of weapon.

But everyone in this video looked so happy, so joyful, that I wanted to be part of it. And as fate would have it, Pub Choir was coming to Chicago – just a few hours away by train – a couple months later.

Pre-pickleball Rick would have swiped right past this video. But having tried this new game and fallen madly in love with it, was I really going to deprive myself of something else I might enjoy? Hell, no. So what if I felt a little embarrassed. Everyone else there would be doing the same embarrassing thing.

As I write this, I've just come back from that Chicago weekend. And you know what? It was a blast. Would I have chosen Whitney Houston's "Dance with Somebody" as the song for that night? I would not. Did I fully commit and yodel out my part as best I could? Absolutely. The moment when all 800 of us finished singing all the way through the first time, the auditorium erupting with delight; it was exactly as joyous as I'd hoped.

Lesson learned: Never, ever shy away from trying something new. I'll leave you with this well-known but decidedly apt quote from Henry David Thoreau:

> *"I went to the woods because I wished to live deliberately, to front only the essential facts of life, and see if I could not learn what it had to teach, and not, when I came to die, discover that I had not lived. I did not wish to live what was not life, living is so dear; nor did I wish to practise resignation, unless it was quite necessary. I wanted to live deep and suck out all the marrow of life…"*

Life is short, folks. Get that marrow.

SAY HELLO

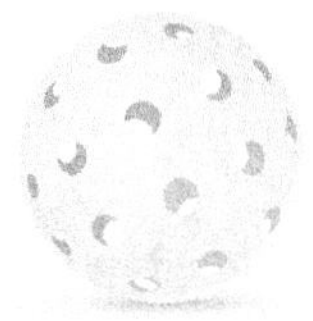

’ve never had a problem speaking in front of large groups, but ask me to strike up a conversation with a stranger? I'm shy and tongue-tied.

This despite growing up with a mother who's a champion at talking to anyone and everyone. Indeed, to this day I am still regaled with stories of people she met on the airplane, in the grocery store, on the phone with tech support when the printer wasn't working. When I was a kid, it embarrassed me when she'd strike up a conversation with a total stranger. Now I genuinely admire this skill, much as I've struggled to learn it. It probably helps explain why Mom has legions of friends, new and old, while I have around three.

On the sidelines of a pickleball court, however, I've found it remarkably easy to engage because there's such a wealth of easy conversation-starters:

"How long have you been playing?"

"Where else do you play?"

"Did you play tennis before this?"

"How do you like that paddle?"

"Not easy playing in this wind, right?"

"Does your significant other play too?" (Single folks, here's your ice-breaker!)

This has proven invaluable to me, because I *suck* at small talk. This common interest, with all its variables and considerations, makes conversation much simpler to kick-start, and that's how friendships are born.

It's also how discoveries are made. A while back I started chatting with a guy named Rob; he looked kind of familiar to me, so I asked how we might know each other.

"What's your last name?" he asked me.

"Broida."

"Oh, you must know Ed Broida."

"That was my dad."

"Was?"

"He passed away last year."

It turned out Rob had worked in the same office, maybe 20 years earlier. Nice guy, newly retired; he said nice things about my dad. That moment of reconnecting to his memory by way of someone who knew him, it was really special. And it wouldn't have happened if I hadn't asked Rob where else he played pickleball.

I'm trying to remember, too, that a lot of people show up for pickleball not just for pickleball, but also for connection. So if I see someone sitting on their own, waiting for a game, I'll strike up a conversation – maybe offer up a little of that connection. I've been on the receiving end of that, and it's really nice. Like, someone noticed me, someone took an interest in me. If ever such a kindness deserved to be paid forward, it's that one.

Here's a great quote; author unknown:

Some stranger, somewhere, still remembers you because you were kind to them when no one else was.

LESSON 3

STOP APOLOGIZING

Early in my pickleball career, I played after-work drop-in games at Scranton Middle School in Brighton, Michigan. Once again I was delighted by the smiling, friendly people I met there: Jay and Sheree, Dan and Tracy, Trudy, Ganesh, Lauren (who I'd later team up with for tournaments), and Wendy.

I have a strong memory of one of my first games at Scranton, when I was still green, still learning the basics. I was playing with Wendy, a retired school principal (and superb player) who couldn't have been nicer and more welcoming.

(In pickleball, especially drop-in, it's quite common to end up partnered with a stranger, which creates a sort of instant kinship. I can't think of another sport that's quite the same in this respect; usually you're part of the same team or at least playing alongside people you know. Pickleball is like speed-dating, in a way. Speed-dinking?)

Early in the game I made some kind of mistake – ball into the net, ball out of bounds, the usual – and said what anyone would say to their partner at such a moment: "Sorry about that!"

Without missing a beat, Wendy answered, "There are no sorrys in pickleball!"

I laughed, but then realized she was serious. And brilliant.

Everyone makes mistakes on the court. Literally everyone, even the pros. And of course you feel bad when you let your partner down, especially with an unforced error. Hence the urge to apologize.

I wondered why we're hardwired this way, why we immediately feel the need to ask forgiveness when all we've done is hit a ball into a net. To find out, I put the question to Dr. Jason Novetsky, Ph.D, a sports psychologist whose clients range from schoolkids to professional athletes.

"We all have this innate sense that we want to belong," he says. "It goes back to caveman days. If we make mistakes, or do something that is detrimental to the family, or the tribe, or the team, there's an innate fear that we're going to be excluded or ostracized."

Sounds about right. I know from excluded and ostracized. (Heck, I'm only three chapters into this book and I already feel like apologizing for it. "Sorry it isn't funnier. Sorry it isn't more insightful. HERE, TAKE YOUR MONEY BACK!")

Here's the thing, though: Your partner probably doesn't expect an apology and won't feel slighted in the slightest about not getting one. "The pitcher doesn't apologize to the shortstop for throwing a bad pitch," Jason says. "Everyone on the team knows that everyone is trying their best; there's never going to be absolute perfection."

I think from Wendy's point of view, it's also about keeping the game going. If you apologize every time you make a mistake, and your partner does likewise, it's going to be a non-stop *Sorry*-fest. The advice is as practical as it is psychologically sound.

So as difficult as it is to suppress the urge to atone for my momentary failure, I find it incredibly liberating to do just that. It gives me mental license to accept the mistake and move on, to know that even if I cost us the point or, worse, the game, it's just part of pickleball.

And life, natch.

I now share this with every partner I have. When someone apologizes to me for a bad play, I repeat Wendy's sage words:

There are no sorrys in pickleball.

STEP OUT OF YOUR COMFORT ZONE

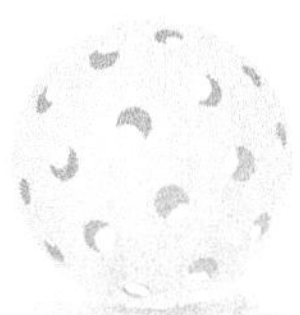

My first pickleball league experience was at The Sports Club of West Bloomfield, which has been around so long it played a small part in my childhood: My dad played tennis there during winter months, and when my mom was busy during league evenings, he'd bring me along and plunk me down to wait. Funny how parents back then didn't concern themselves with their children's boredom. I have no idea what I did to occupy myself during those hours, especially after the quarters ran out and all I could do was stare wistfully at the Ms. Pac-Man and Crazy Climber arcade machines.

I mention that only because I felt a bit of nostalgia walking in those doors. But even more amazing was what came after that.

This was a six-week mixed ladder league, meaning you'd get assigned to a particular court for the week and play a fixed number of games there, switching partners after each one. Whoever had the highest score for that week would move up a court; the lowest-scoring player would move down one. Eventually this "sorting hat" system would result in fairly even matches across the lineup.

I liked this arrangement because it allowed me to play with lots of different partners, some a bit stronger, some a bit weaker, but always changing from one game to the next.

Eventually I made my way to the top two courts, where for several weeks I played with and against the same handful of people: Amy, Sherrie, Barry, Marty, Nancy, and Jodi, to name a few. All great players, all friendly and welcoming and fun to hang with for a couple hours each week.

With the session coming to an end, however, and indoor play largely wrapping up for the winter, what next? I'd likely never see these people again, or at least not until next fall.

You've heard this countless times before: It's really difficult for adults to make new friends. Part of the reason is lack of opportunity, because outside of work (assuming you even go to an office anymore), where do you meet people?

Duh: The pickleball court! That not only satisfied the "where" problem, but also overcame the obstacle of finding something you have in common.

Okay, but how to take the *next* step? How could I turn these court acquaintances into actual friends?

As fate (or maybe a TikTok video) would have it, I'd just learned about a book called *The 2-Hour Cocktail Party*, by Nick Gray. In it he describes the value of such gatherings – meeting new people, strengthening relationships – and the steps to make them happen.

I consulted with my wife, the most amazing and supportive woman on the planet, and she was all for it – despite the scary prospect of inviting a bunch of strangers into the house who all have something in common that she doesn't. (Hey, I'd like nothing more than for us to be one of those couples who play pickleball together, but for the moment she's not into it. I'll keep working on her. No one escapes the cult.)

So I ginned up an invitation, printed copies on card stock, and brought them to the final week of the league. They looked like this:

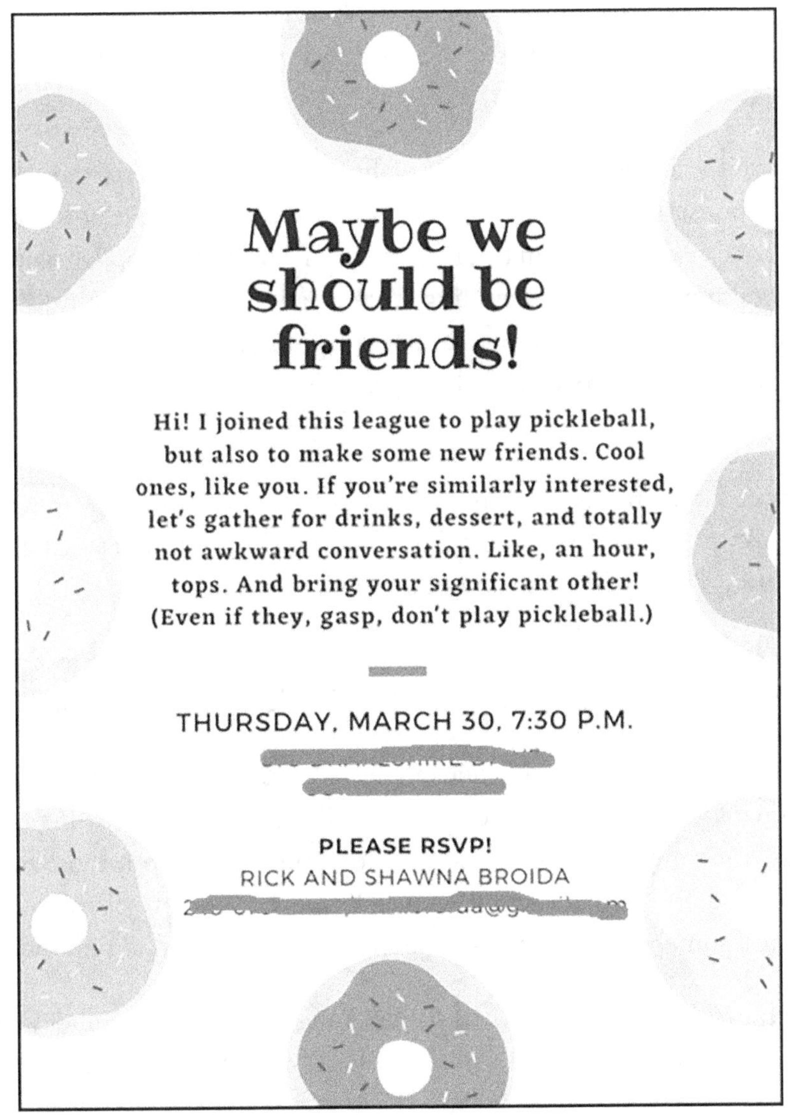

I know: pretty dorky. (Full disclosure: So am I.) I was incredibly nervous when I handed these out after the session. My expectation was a lot of strange looks followed by "I'll have to check my calendar" followed by "Thanks but we're busy that day."

To my amazement, the invitations were met with delight. "I feel like I just got invited to a bar mitzvah!" Sherrie exclaimed. Jodi noted it was "so nice to get an invitation to something." (Remember, this was still early days after the Pandemic.)

And you know what? Out of the eight people I invited, six came (with their spouses). They stayed for two hours instead of one, and I think everyone had a good time. I'm not sure I consumed enough wine to fully calm my nerves that evening, but overall it was a success. And I was deeply gratified that everyone seemed so appreciative. Because how often do you get invited to a cocktail party anymore? I think people miss these kinds of get-togethers.

Now, if I'm being totally honest, the party produced exactly zero lasting friendships. I still bump into a few of these folks from time to time, and I'm always happy to see them (and vice-versa, I hope).

That's okay! The "win" for me was stepping outside my comfort zone, doing something that terrified me at a DNA level but doing it anyway.

About a year after this, I found myself on the receiving end of a similar invitation: Rick Fernandez (who you'll meet later) invited me to his house for a guys' night of pizza and ping-pong. I love both those things but was pretty nervous about going. Would I know any of the others? What if somebody started talking politics? What if I lost at ping-pong?

But how often do I get invited to just hang out with some dudes? Not too often. I was happy to be asked. So I put my fears aside and accepted.

And my fears were, as usual, unjustified. All the guys: cool.

Politics talk: none.

Ping-pong: skills intact; never lost a game. (Still waiting on my medal, Fernandez.)

I'm beginning to think my comfort zone is an idiot. Or, at a minimum, that comfort is overrated.

I'll leave you with this quote from *Finding Nemo*, spoken by Dory to Nemo's dad:

> *Well, you can't never let anything happen to him. Then nothing would ever happen to him. Not much fun for little Harpo.*

DON'T JUDGE A BOOK...

In 2023 I visited my mom in Florida, where she lived in a massive gated community with a very active pickleball crowd.

As fate would have it, the weekend of my visit coincided with a "member/guest" tournament, meaning residents could partner with visiting friends or family members. Although Mom wasn't a player herself, she had a friend there who needed a "guest."

And so I was introduced to a woman I'll call Sally, who texted me instructions on how to find her on the courts the morning of the tournament: "Look for the lady with braces on both elbows and both knees."

Ho, boy. Well, hey, this is just for fun, right? So what if I have to do the heavy lifting for my mid-70s partner with the bum joints?

Sure enough, she was easy to spot when I got there; there are plenty of arm and leg braces to be found on Florida pickleball courts, but not many players rocking the quad-fecta.

If I had any concerns about Sally's skills, they were quickly dispelled; she proved as strong a player as anyone out there. In fact, after seven games, we'd lost only one; another victory and we'd be tied for first place.

I liked our chances. Our final game was against two, um, *older* gentlemen (I was going to say "geezers" but that seems disrespectful – accurate, but disrespectful). They looked like they'd needed scooters just to reach the court. Both in their 80s, one carrying considerable weight around the midsection, one who looked like he might struggle just to raise his arms over his head.

Piece of cake.

You know where this is going. A lesson most of us learn early in life: Don't judge a book by its cover. There's the literal truth to this – I would have bypassed *This Tender Land* by William Kent Krueger based on the "unmanly" title alone, but I'd have missed out on a genuinely fabulous book – and there's the pickleball version: You don't play for long before you learn not to judge players by their age, appearance, or quantity of joint-relief accoutrements. Sally had already surprised me with her skills, but that was nothing compared to our game against Statler and Waldorf. (That's a *Muppets* reference, kids; look it up.)

They whipped us. I mean, it wasn't even close. At one point I mumbled to Sally, "How are we losing to these two?"

This wasn't a random occurrence. I've faced off against heavyset guys who looked like they'd never heard of the gym, let alone been inside one – and got my butt handed to me. I've played with frail-looking older ladies who hit impossibly well-placed shots, and did so consistently.

Yes, I'm the idiot here. I know it's human nature to make assessments about people based on the way they look or talk, but time and again my assessments have proven wrong. And for whatever reason, pickleball has driven the point home in a way that other situations haven't. I now feel I'm doing better at avoiding snap judgments off the court, and feel better for having made that mental adjustment.

There's an offshoot lesson here as well: Don't judge yourself by your own cover. You might think you're not skilled or athletic enough to play pickleball, especially when you see experienced players go at it, but chances are good you're wrong. It's not a hard game! The court is small, so there's not much running (especially at the beginner level). And in the end, all you have to do is hit that ball over the net. Before you judge yourself out of even trying, get out there and play.

I'll leave you with this quote from a particularly wise Muppet who lived a long time ago in a galaxy far, far away…

Size matters not. Judge me by my size, do you?

The Original 'Pickle Rick'

The day I met Rick Fernandez, he kind of ticked me off. This was at Legacy Sports Complex in Brighton, Michigan, one of the few places (at the time) I could find an indoor game during the cold winter months. I was still a relative rookie when I showed up for drop-in play, but thus far had encountered only the friendly, encouraging people I've alluded to before.

Rick was friendly enough when we were partnered together for a game, but it wasn't long before unsolicited advice started coming my way. When I let a lob go past my head because I thought sure it was going long (it didn't), he said, "Ohh, come on, partner, you gotta hit those." When I sent an easy volley into the net, he chided: "Can't miss the easy ones."

I later came to understand that Rick wasn't criticizing me; he was joking with me. I was so self-conscious at the time, still feeling like a beginner, that I took it personally. Before long I got to know him much better, to the point where I'm now comfortable returning the smack-talk he throws my way. He's an incredibly good doubles player, still winning tournaments, and not too shabby at singles, either (though we both know who usually wins when we play).

Rick now runs the entire pickleball program at Legacy. He's genuinely enthusiastic about helping others learn to play, which tells you everything you need to know. Pickleball made a huge impact in his life, and he's happy to pay it forward.

It's especially fun to play against Rick and his partner Ernie (who you'll meet shortly) – not because it's all but guaranteed they'll smoke you (nothing fun about that), but because they're hilarious together. If pickleball had a Vaudeville act, it'd be these two. The way they trade barbs with each other – who was responsible for that lost point, who's "carrying" the other – is genuinely entertaining. If you've ever seen Steve Martin and Martin Short together, it's like that – but on a pickleball court.

Rick has never self-identified as "Pickle Rick," which is fine because I'd rather use that moniker myself as I rise to pickleball book author fame and glory. But "other Rick" (or "bad Rick," as Ernie often refers to him now) definitely deserves some recognition. He's a class act.

(And don't worry, guys, I'm not going to mention the time Jim and I beat you 11-0. That's called "getting pickled," but I'm sure most readers are already familiar with that terminology. No need to discuss it here.)

BE GRACIOUS

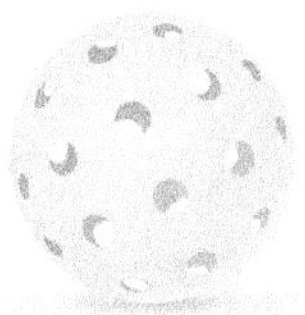

In my early days on the court, I approached pickleball the same way I'd approached tennis, basketball, and other sports: Play to win, dominate at all costs. Your opponent isn't your friend; he's your obstacle, and you treat him accordingly.

Imagine my surprise, then, upon being complimented for a winning shot. ("Wow, too good, Rick.") Or encouraged when making a bad one. ("Oh, that was so close!") And this was coming from the *other* side of the net. What the heck was going on here? Were these people playing head games with me?

The *esprit-de-corps* in pickleball is just bonkers. (*Esprit-de*-court, more like.)

Over time, my reflexive response shifted. When an opposing player hit a winner, I might get momentarily angry with myself (or, ahem, my partner) for letting it happen, but I'd also instinctively share a compliment: "That was *nice*." "Great shot." "Ya got me!"

Indeed, for the first time in my life, I managed to surrender to the fun of the sport. Sure, I still whack my thigh with the paddle when I send an easy dink into the net or a serve out of bounds. But I never lose patience with my partner because, well, *I* sometimes send an easy dink into the net or a serve out of bounds.

More to the point, I genuinely love it when an opposing player hits a great shot. Okay, maybe not *love*, but I recognize and appreciate the skill. Recently I played a game against Tracy, a league regular who tends to be especially hard on herself. (Tracy: See Lesson 8.) The thing is, she's a crackerjack player, routinely hitting winning punch-volleys at the net and perfectly placed lobs from the baseline.

During one point, I was at the net when she sent a ball over my head (not easy, because I'm tall and pretty quick on my feet). I was sure it was going long, so I didn't backpedal to chase it. But it landed right in the corner, perfect placement; point, Tracy. And I broke out in a big smile and gave her a well-deserved "paddle clap," because I was just so impressed by her shot. I didn't feel badly I'd lost the point; I felt glad she'd hit such a beautiful lob.

This mindset does *not* come naturally to me. But it calls to mind the old saying: A rising tide lifts all boats. The nicer people are to me, the nicer I want to be to others. Even if I lose a game, a match, a tournament, I feel good about congratulating my opponents because I know it'll help make them feel good, and because I've been on the other side of that goodwill.

Maybe the more relevant saying is one from my mom: It's nice to be nice.

The famous football coach Knute Rockne said, "Show me a good and gracious loser and I'll show you a failure." Wrong, sir. I'll take my inspiration from singer Stevie Nicks instead:

> *Your graciousness is what carries you. If you are gracious, you have won the game.*

DON'T GIVE UP

It pains me to admit this in public, but I'm a notorious giver-upper. I'm easily frustrated and discouraged; if something is tedious or difficult, I'll typically quit it rather than persevere.

Indeed, I've unwittingly subscribed to the Homer Simpson philosophy of life, which he once summarized thusly to a discouraged Bart:

> *Son, come here. Of course I'm not mad. If something's hard to do, then it's not worth doing. You just stick that guitar in the garage next to your short-wave radio, your karate outfit, and your unicycle, and we'll go and watch TV.*

Ironically, I'm writing this not four feet from the guitar I wish-listed for my 40th birthday, the one I abandoned after a few lessons because, it turns out, guitar is *hard*. It now hangs on the wall as a bit of décor, where it taunts me daily. (Note to self: Take down the Shrine of Failure.)

In pickleball, it's easy to get frustrated and discouraged, especially when you're seemingly overmatched on the court. When you're down 8-1 in a game to 11 and the other team still has the serve, it's only natural to think, "Well, that's that." Concede defeat, let the last few points slide, get it over with so you can move on to the next game.

But here's the thing: I've been down 8-1 in a game to 11 and come back to win it. I've also been on the other side of a huge lead and managed to blow it. In both cases, it was because no one gave up.

There are countless examples of this across all sports. In 2022, the Minnesota Vikings were down 33-0 in the third quarter. Any fans who left the stadium because, well, *game over*, missed the greatest comeback in NFL history. Led by former Michigan State quarterback Kirk Cousins (go Green!), the Vikings won the day in overtime, 39-36.

In 2004, the Boston Red Sox were down 3-0 in the World Series, meaning the championship was all but decided; no team had ever come back from that kind of deficit. The Sox swept the next four games and won it all.

Maybe I should pick up that guitar again. Or at least the 50th-birthday ukelele that's hanging right next to it. (I thought it would be easier!)

I'll leave you with this quote from renowned columnist Marilyn vos Savant:

> *Being defeated is often a temporary condition. Giving up is what makes it permanent.*

Ernie

It was Rick who introduced me to Ernie Miller, his doubles partner; they'd met at a singles tournament, taken first and second place, and become fast friends. Most recently they'd taken gold together in the local Senior Olympics and were currently mowing down the competition in a Brighton city league. Once again, my first impression wasn't the best; Ernie speaks in a slow, deliberate drawl and says things like, "I hit balls out, but I don't hit out-balls" (in reference to your last mishit). But I quickly learned that this is his brand of deadpan comedy. He's like Don Rickles without the meanness; even when he's directing his barbs at you, you can't help but laugh. When your team loses the serve in quick succession and the ball goes back to Ernie's side, he'll ask very earnestly: "Did you guys serve yet? OK, just checking."

Not long after we met, I ran into him at the singles tournament I mentioned at the beginning of the book. He'd accidentally arrived too early for his bracket, so he had lots of time to kill. We chatted a bit; I told him I was extremely new to singles pickleball and this was my first tournament. He told me he'd played college tennis, which helped me understand his 4.0+ skills. (Wait, they had tennis in the 1800s?)

In between my games I'd see Ernie sitting on the sidelines, wandering here and there, idly waiting for his bracket to begin. Eventually I started my final match; I was 3-0 for the day, and so was my opponent. This was for all the marbles. I was exhausted; there was too much downtime between games and my muscles were getting tight. I started out losing; I was outmatched and pretty sure the handwriting was on the wall.

But then, somehow, I battled back and won. As I came off the court, shaking my head in disbelief, I spied Ernie across the arena. He looked at me questioningly: Was it over? Involuntarily, I threw my hands over my head. Victory! And Ernie, who I barely knew, who barely knew me, threw *his* hands over his head and broke out in a huge smile. Warm, enthusiastic congratulations followed. Deadpan Ernie, the big bear, was genuinely happy for me. I've never forgotten that.

Months later, he asked me to join him in a 4.0 tournament, filling in for Fernandez, who was out of town. Big shoes to fill, and I felt I was more of a 3.5 player, but I said yes (and couldn't help but mention the value of this "Rick upgrade"). The day arrived, and we lost our first two games. I was nervous, not playing well. I didn't want to disappoint Ernie, who isn't accustomed to losing. Then, mid-way through our third game, I settled down and turned it around; we came from behind and won it. Then we won our next three in a row and somehow walked away with silver for the day.

I felt bad about the rocky start, but if Ernie was miffed about not taking the gold, he didn't show it. Indeed, he was all smiles; he stuffed his bag with cookies from the snack table and headed home. In the weeks that followed I heard over and over, as Ernie recounted the tournament to others, that "Rick is a great player — after he gets in three warm-up games." Months later, a *year* later, I continue to hear variations on this refrain. "Rick, did you play your warm-up games yet?" Once Ernie has your "story" locked in, it's on permanent repeat. He has not forgotten our tournament together. He probably never will.

And I'll still laugh every time.

FORGIVE YOUR MISTAKES

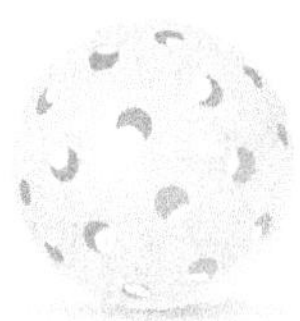

Even with nearly three years' worth of leagues, tournaments, and drop-in games under my belt, I make mistakes on the court. *Lots* of them. And I still struggle to control my temper, which explains why my right thigh is often red after a game. (A few chastising whacks with the paddle will do that.)

I'm highly competitive, always have been. There's no psychology degree hanging on my wall, but I'm fairly certain that that competitiveness comes from personal insecurity: I feel like if I lose, at *anything*, I'm going to be the target of laughter, mockery, maybe outright bullying – all of which I experienced as a kid.

Even after I stopped apologizing to my partner, I still got angry when I played poorly. (It's crazy to me how you can nail every shot one day and then send easy ones into the net the next!)

Once again I asked sports-psychologist Jason Novetsky for some insight. How do athletes learn to forgive themselves, to move on past these moments of defeat?

"I believe that before forgiveness comes acceptance," he told me. "Going into any competition or performance, one must first accept that mistakes or bad shots will happen and understand that no matter what happens, they will ultimately be okay. Once we accept the potential outcomes, it's much easier to forgive oneself."

Not long ago I played a mixed-doubles tournament that did *not* go well. Although my partner and I had scored gold in a previous tournament, we lost five out of six games that afternoon.

After the last of them, I was *pissed*. I'd made a ton of mistakes; so had she. We just didn't play well. Without a word, I stormed off the court, about to spiral further into anger, embarrassment, self-loathing – the usual.

But then something remarkable happened: I got over it. I reminded myself that I didn't single-handedly cost us our medal; we lost as a team. What's more, the competition out there was *fierce*; maybe what I interpreted as playing poorly was simply getting out-played.

Then I remembered that I'd hit some good shots, too. Strong serves, a few winners, that nice hard-slice backhand that zoomed straight up the middle, neither opponent able to reach it.

I also recalled that I'd played really well the day before in the men's tournament, beating tough teams I was sure would destroy us.

And the big one: I freed myself from the thinking that everyone – that *anyone* – was judging my performance. The other players in the tournament? They only cared about their games. The handful of spectators on the sidelines? Did I honestly think they were pointing and laughing? Who knows if they were even watching me, and even if they were, so what? They were strangers; they didn't know me, and I didn't know them.

When I say this was remarkable, I mean it. Somehow, in the span of just a couple minutes, I managed to calm down and forgive myself. To remember that it's just a game, that I came here to have fun and get exercise, that I already have some medals hanging up at home. Did it matter if I wasn't collecting another one that day? It did not.

"Obviously this is a healthier way to enjoy our sports or performances," Jason said – and that was before this particular tournament. He meant that *we will make mistakes*, and it's both okay and acceptable.

I need to work on remembering this beforehand, so I can better forgive myself during games and not let mistakes derail my performance.

But that day I felt glad I'd remembered it at all, because it helped me keep my confidence going into the second half of the men's tournament later that same day – and collect a bronze medal in the process. (*See*, Rick? Sometimes you win.)

This is one of the biggest life-lessons I've extracted from pickleball, the realization that everyone makes mistakes and the only mistake that matters is dwelling on them. Countless times in life I've put my foot in my mouth – no, swallowed it whole – and spent months, *years*, dwelling on it. But that's because I chose to do so; I allowed myself to carry those memories and feel embarrassed or ashamed by them.

So enough already. If I can dust myself off on the pickleball court, if I can forgive missing that easy dink and just move on to the next point, I can stop stressing out about that dumb thing I said 10 years ago – that dumb thing no one remembers except me.

Tennis legend Jim Courier had this to say:

> *Sportsmanship for me is when a guy walks off the court and you really can't tell whether he won or lost, when he carries himself with pride either way.*

My Worst Pickleball Moments

With all the gushing I've done about pickleball, you'd think it's been nothing but sunshine and lollipops. Not quite.

There are two memories that continue to gnaw at me, times when I let my mouth get me into trouble the way it has so many times before. I try not to dwell on them, try to follow my own advice, but these two are a struggle.

The first took place during a highly competitive men's league. I was rotating my way through a round-robin with a bunch of guys I didn't know well. They all seemed friendly enough with each other, but because I was new to that court that week, they didn't know me. Odd man out.

A few games in, my partner and I found ourselves losing big; I think the score was 8-1 or maybe even 9-0. But, hey: Lesson 7. Don't give up! We didn't, and soon enough we were tied and then leading. Feeling pretty jazzed about the comeback, I grinned and said to my partner, "Ohhh, this is gonna hurt!" By which I meant it was going to suck for the other team to lose after having such a huge lead.

From across the net I heard, "That was a dickish thing to say." Then, after the game was over (we did indeed win), we all tapped paddles and the other guy said it again to my face: "That was a really dickish thing to say."

I was crushed. I'd just been caught up in the moment and trying to be funny. Like Rick or Ernie would have. But I'd failed to read the room. I wasn't playing a casual game with buddies; I was playing on court one with guys who didn't know me, didn't know my sense of humor, and definitely didn't want to lose after being up nine points.

I mumbled an apology and headed for the sidelines, sure that this guy was now running me down to everyone else on the court. *Did you hear what that asshole said during our game?* Every childhood insecurity came flooding back. They'd all make fun of me. They'd intentionally lose games to get me knocked down a court. No more warm welcomes; now I'd be lucky to get a "Hey." One stupid, ill-timed joke and I'd become a pickleball pariah.

But then, to my surprise, it seemed to blow over. A few minutes later I saw the guy chatting and laughing, sending zero glares in my direction. And as we were packing up our stuff, I said, "Hey, man, sorry again. Just a dumb joke." He nodded and waved it off; no harm, no foul.

Even so, I moped over this for days after, because my brain likes to punish me. Was it really a "dickish" remark? Or was the guy fuming over the fact that he'd blown a huge lead, and this felt like pouring salt in the wound? No doubt some of both. I did my best to forgive myself, to remember that it's okay if someone is mad at me or even doesn't like me.

But, wow, that was just a warm-up for my next exciting foot-in-mouth adventure. In one fell swoop I managed to get two people mad at me, one of whom almost took a swing.

It's a mixed-doubles tournament; I'm playing with my partner Lauren, with whom I'd won gold in our previous outing. We were gunning for another medal.

In one of our games, we squared off against a rather odd couple: An older woman, maybe early 60s, and a young, heavyset guy I guessed to be in his late teens. They were a formidable pair; she was unbeatable at the net ("Don't judge a book!"), and he fired cannon blasts from the baseline.

We were losing, and I was getting frustrated – not because of the score, but because this kid, who I'll call Jake, was obnoxious. Every time they'd win a point, he'd raise his fist and yell, "Yeaaahhhh!!!" Like it was some colossal victory. That's fine if you hit a really great shot, but to do it after practically every point? And especially when the opposing team (*us*) makes a mistake? Not cool.

Between points I said to Lauren, "This is really pissing me off." She agreed; it was annoying her, too. A point or two later, after another big "Yeaaaahh!", I approached the net and said, "Hey, man, that's really bad sportsmanship."

"I can say whatever I want!" he replied.

"I know you can, and I'll telling you that when you yell like that after every point, it's bad sportsmanship."

A few more words – fairly heated – were exchanged along the same lines, then play resumed. And we came back. And won. The kid's game had fallen apart; he'd obviously been rattled by what I'd said, lost his confidence.

At the post-game paddle-tap, I tried to make amends: "Hey, man, no harm, no foul."

He glared at me. "Whatever. I can say what I want." And he stormed off.

A few minutes later I'm courtside waiting for our team's next match-up. Suddenly a man is in my face. "Hey! What the hell are you doing, yelling at a kid?"

Shocked by this, I mumbled something along the lines of, "He was being a bad sport."

"He's 17 years old!" the guy yelled.

Now I'm getting a little irritated. "What business is it of yours?"

"I'm his father!" he roars. "You're damn right it's my business!" He turns to leave, then turns back and makes a motion toward me, like he's expecting me to flinch. I don't, because I'm still rather incredulous that this is happening and because I've got about three inches on this guy. (And I kickbox.)

Finally he stomps off. The tournament ends; Lauren and I take fourth, the kid and his partner end up third. Had they beaten us, they'd have scored silver.

This happened well over a year ago; I still find myself ruminating on it. (Remember: I have punish-brain.) Was I right to call this kid out on his bad behavior? I feel like lots of players in my position would have done the same (and not given it a second thought, honestly). Was I wrong to do it in the middle of tournament game instead of after the fact? I think yes, absolutely.

All I know is, I have to walk around knowing Jake and his father hate my guts. I've since crossed paths with Jake in some league games, even played alongside him, and tried my best to put it behind us. I pay him compliments when appropriate; he says almost nothing to me.

I get it. From his perspective, he got chewed out in public for being, well, himself. Right or wrong, that's a terrible thing for a 17-year-old to endure. Been there, endured that. I'm sorry, Jake. I truly am.

BE A GENTLEMAN (OR A LADY)

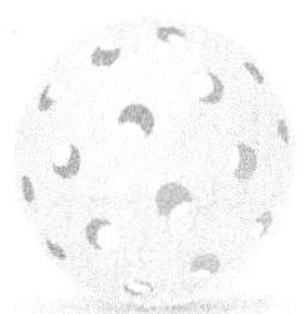

I've played in mixed leagues and men's leagues, and the difference between them is striking. The men behave like, well, men: Some talk very little, some get hotheaded, a few let competitiveness get in the way of a good time. Others are jovial and jokey; you've already met Ernie, who somehow manages to make you laugh even while he's whipping you. (And then again after he's done whipping you. And when he reminds you of the whipping weeks later.)

The ladies, on the other hand, are almost always more social. (I know: shocker!) They laugh, they compliment and encourage each other, they have *fun*. There are some competitive women on the court, absolutely, but generally speaking, I find they're just there to have a good time. And it's infectious: I've found I'm much more relaxed in a mixed-doubles game, probably because I don't feel the same pressure to win (and don't feel like I'm going to get chastised if I make a bad shot).

But, oh, how I feel for the ladies paired with mansplainers (whether they're spouses, friends, or total strangers), who can't stop themselves telling their partner where to stand, how to hit, and what they did wrong. Who poach at the net instead of letting her take the volley. Guys, I know you want to win, but don't suck the fun out of it for your partner.

This can go both ways. In my earlier days of playing in leagues, when I was still tentative and unsure, I found myself partnered with a woman who, before the game began, marched up and launched into a game-plan diatribe. She told me how she was going to play and how I should play. During the game she told me what I was doing wrong. (Never mind that she made plenty of her own mistakes.)

She did all this because she wanted to win, which I get. But her instructions and critiques made me incredibly self-conscious, making me feel worse about my performance. Plus, we're partners! We're supposed to build each other up. I was so taken aback by her words – no, just plain angry – I almost wanted us to lose the game, just so she'd be pissed, too.

I feel like the pickleball court should be a safe space, a place you go to have fun without fear of criticism or recrimination. And that means not being a critic. Or a loudmouth. Maybe leave home the political hats and t-shirts, too.

One thing that struck me early on: I rarely hear anyone cursing on the pickleball court. You'd think that in a game where there's so much error, there'd be so much profanity. I'm not saying I never hear an F-bomb (starting with the ones muttered under my own breath), merely that there's a surprising level of calm on the court. I've seen surprisingly few tempers flare. Mostly I hear laughter and whoops of delight (like when a ball hits the tape at the top of the net and slooowly dribbles over).

I do have a story, though: My local league play often puts me in the path of Dot (not her real name), and her temper is legendary. The expletives fly fast and loud; I can hear her cry "Oh, *SHIT!*" from three courts away.

Typically this leads to an exchange of amused looks with other players; Dot is an otherwise kind and reserved lady, but once she gets on the court and makes a few mistakes, she could make a sailor blush.

Once again, I get it. It can be frustrating when you're not playing well and embarrassing because you feel like you're letting your partner down.

And who knows what Dot's life is like off the court? Maybe she hates her job. Maybe her partner is super-critical of her. Maybe she's just like me, deeply insecure and hyper-sensitive about failing in front of others.

But she's the exception, not the rule. I think it's because pickleball is so social and so fun, the good times outweigh the ephemeral screw-ups. (For most of us.)

My dad taught me to hold the door for others. My mom taught me that if someone in the car ahead of you is driving slowly, maybe it's because there's a cake in the backseat. Pickleball merges these two lessons: Help your partner, and be understanding because you don't know what's going on in someone else's life. Maybe they have a cake in the car.

I'll leave you with this quote from American economist Thomas Sowell:

> *Politeness and consideration for others is like investing pennies and getting dollars back.*

DON'T BELIEVE EVERYTHING YOU READ (EXCEPT THIS, OBVIOUSLY)

By now you've probably seen articles warning of the "huge growth in pickleball-related injuries." Play this sport at your own peril, these stories suggest; emergency rooms have been *flooded* with twisted ankles, torn rotator cuffs, strained knees, and horrific ball-induced bruises.

Oh, *no*! I better stay home, then.

Except pickleball may be the least dangerous sport since shuffleboard. Do you run around a bit? Sure. Are arms and elbows involved? Of course. Is the ball occasionally hit hard in the direction of your face or body? Yep.

Obviously when you start playing a new sport – any new sport – there's a chance you might incur a twist or sprain. And when millions of people start playing a new sport, the injury count goes up accordingly.

But that's not what news organizations like to report. Instead, headlines blare about the pickleball injury *epidemic*. The game is inherently dangerous; it's the *deep dark secret no one talks about*.

But that's ridiculous. If millions of people suddenly started playing pinochle, we'd be inundated with stories about repetitive-strain wrist injuries from dealing all those cards.

For years I've been frustrated by the media's handling of health news; some new study comes out and suddenly coffee is bad for you, never mind the fact that it was conducted on 28 people and sponsored by the tea industry. (Gotta watch Big Tea; they'll stop at nothing.)

Remember how eggs were going to kill us all? That was the conventional wisdom for decades, until suddenly eggs were okay again. Better than okay; they have protein! And by the way you need *way more protein in your diet*. (For now; by my estimate the protein backlash starts in 5, 4, 3…)

Modern journalism is rife with click-bait headlines, to say nothing of poorly researched or woefully incomplete stories. And this is only going to get worse as AI starts generating news articles and fact-checking falls by the wayside.

So I guess I already knew this lesson, but I wanted to share it anyway. I roll my eyes every time I see a "pickleball injuries on the rise" headline because I know that although it's true, it's not the whole story. Not even close.

(That being said, I urge you to spend 5-10 minutes warming up before you hit the court – something I rarely see players do. A few minutes of dinking is *not* a warm-up; you need to get the blood flowing – I like jumping-jacks but you can also do high-knees marching in place – and loosen up those calves, shoulders, neck muscles, and so on. A quick Google search will reveal plenty of pickleball-specific warm-up exercises.)

My favorite quote on this subject, by far, was found online:

> *Don't believe everything you read on the Internet.* –Abraham Lincoln

Got Muscle Cramps? This Home Remedy Will Shock You!

Yeah, that's exactly the kind of clickbait headline I'm talking about. Except this one, well, might actually be true.

Because here's a true story: I played in a singles tournament that lasted a good three-plus hours. I drank electrolytes and water all throughout, so although I was pretty exhausted at the end, I didn't feel dehydrated.

A few minutes after falling into bed that evening, I felt a cramp building in my leg. If you've ever had muscle cramps of any kind, you know they're horrific. I've learned how to stretch out a foot or calf when this happens, but this one was on the side, to the left of my shin – new to me, and there didn't seem to be a stretch that could relieve it.

I grabbed my phone, searched for "fast leg-cramp relief," and landed on an article that would have made me laugh out loud if not for the considerable pain.

Stumbling downstairs, I flung open the fridge, hoping to find the prescribed remedy. And there it was, a brand new, unopened jar of... pickles.

I swear I'm not making this up.

Apparently pickle juice is a fairly well-known cure for muscle cramps. At that point I'd have downed a liver-and-blue-cheese smoothie if it meant stopping the pain, so I popped the pickle-jar lid and gulped some of the salty brine.

Cramps: Gone. In an instant. Like magic. Whaaaat.

The science behind this isn't fully understood – it could be the juice's acetic acid signaling nerve receptors, it could be the electrolytes – but I was awfully glad it worked. For me, at least. In that moment.

This is, of course, purely anecdotal. But also purely hilarious. Because pickle juice to help with a pickleball-related ailment? Come on. What's next, a banana-peel bandage when you slip and fall?

PIVOT!

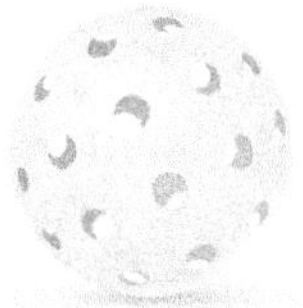

I've never been good at strategizing. Meal-planning, wardrobe selection, whatever's coming out of my mouth next. But especially in sports, when I'm usually fighting fatigue and my own hyper-critical brain. (*You knew that ball had backspin and you still hit it into the net?! What, is this your first day on the court?*) I typically just go from one point to the next, never stopping to actually consider what's happening.

During my conversation with Dr. Novetsky, when we were talking about failure and how to recover from it, he mentioned how one particular pro-athlete reacts during a game that's not going well.

He pivots. Instead of letting the fear of failure creep in and further hobble his performance, he asks himself a simple question: "What to do I need to do to beat this guy?"

In other words, he course-corrects. He adapts to the circumstances he's facing in this game, right here, right now.

Maybe this is Sports 101, but it's a lesson I was never taught. During a recent men's tournament, when we were losing a game I felt we should be winning, I asked myself that very same question: "What do I need to do to beat this team?" And then I asked my partner, "What do *we* need to do to beat this team?"

My partner, Steve, looked at me like I had a pickleball for a head and said, "Stop hitting the ball into the fucking net, for one thing."

Steve may be slightly less philosophical than I am.

We came back and won that game, though I can't say it was because we stopped missing easy shots. I just know that for me, this little pivot – this adapting to the circumstance at hand – enabled me to get out of my head. I stopped criticizing myself for making mistakes, stopped thinking Steve hated me, and started focusing on what needed to be done. Why *were* so many balls going into the net? Because the other team hit with a lot of backspin. How do you compensate for backspin? Bend the knees, get under the ball, swing low to high.

And, surprise, surprise, this works off the pickleball court as well. Flight got cancelled? Forget stomping and stewing; what do I need to do to get rebooked? Boss pointed out something I screwed up? Don't take it personally or threaten to quit; figure out what's needed to make sure it doesn't happen again.

In other words: pivot. Not just in my actions, but in my thinking as well.

Take it from author Robert Greene:

> *Become fluid and flexible, like water, and you will never be thwarted by the unexpected.*

PATIENCE REALLY IS A VIRTUE

It's often said that pickleball is won at the net. Indeed, many points are decided by a dink rally, in which teams try to hit gentle shots into the non-volley zone – the "kitchen" – on the other side of the net.

I'm not great at this, and it's not because I lack the skill to give the ball a light tap with my paddle. It's because I lack patience. I want to win the point, *now*, not wait out a mistake by the other team. And so I get aggressive, trying to score a winner and invariably hitting the ball into the net or popping it up so the other team gets an easy smash.

I've taken exactly one pickleball lesson in my life, taught by the talented Tracy Bruletti, and during a dinking exercise, I told her of this shortcoming. Her response: "Yeah, everyone does that. But nine times out of ten, if you just keep dinking, the other team will make a mistake. They should call it Patience-ball."

Then she chuckled at her own joke, which she'd made up on the spot. Patience-ball. Love it.

I called this to mind when our 30-year-old microwave died and the replacement wouldn't fit properly in the space above the stove: The tile backsplash went up too high for the new bracket to be installed. Suddenly this easy one-hour project had turned into an all-day, might-never-get-done train wreck.

Old Rick's impatience reared up mightily. This extra tile has to be cut away; it's going to take forever. What if the microwave still doesn't fit? I've already tossed all the packaging; how do I return it to the store?

Patience-ball. One step at a time. Do I know anyone who has experience working with tile? Uncle Jack! Is he willing to help? He is! If we take turns with the angle grinder, will we eventually cut through that insanely hard ceramic?

We will.

It took hours, but we got there. Every step of the way, I reminded myself of the need to be patient. Just like at the net. It's difficult, but necessary.

Mahatma Gandhi shared these insightful words on the subject:

> *To lose patience is to lose the battle.*

A Newbie's Guide to Pickleball
By Sarah Broida

It may seem the height of nepotism to give your daughter a corner of your book, but when mine announced she wanted to share her own perspective, how could I refuse? While I'm years into my pickleball journey, Sarah just started hers. And she's not "just" my daughter; she's a creative-genius 4.0-GPA grad student who's already mastered her lob. If you're new to the game, get ready for some seriously astute insights.

Over the past few years, I watched my dad fall in love with this sport, adding it to the *extensive* list of things he's talented at. *[Smart move, starting with the compliments. -Ed.]* After a lot of encouragement (or pushiness, depending on your perspective), my husband, Chase, and I picked up the sport too.

To my surprise (maybe even a little annoyance – "Dad was right!"), I've fallen in love with pickleball as well. Not quite as much – I haven't written an entire book about it – but still. When he writes about the unique vibe that emanates from the court – the camaraderie, the light-heartedness, the moments of excitement – I must admit I've noticed the same thing. It's just... different.

After only a few months of playing, I agreed to enter a tournament with Chase. It didn't go well; we got pickled more than once. Still, I was impressed by other players' abilities, their varying techniques and serves, and learned just how tough the competition can be out there. That said, it sucked to lose – our games all ended way too quickly. I wanted to shout across the net, "I know I'm not actually at your level – I'm a seat filler!" So, yeah, it was a long, tough morning. But despite all that, I kept playing. And eventually joined a league. And then a new indoor facility. There's something about this sport, I can't deny it.

I won't go so far as to say I learned *everything* I need to know from pickleball, but I learned two things. Two sub-lessons, if you will.

Sub-Lesson 1: It's more mental than you think.

It's common knowledge that games, physical or not, require you to think. Strategize. Problem-solve. But those types of thinking are focused on the game, not on you. And what about how you think before and after the games, and how it might affect the outcome? That's where psychology comes into play. (I should know; I graduated college with a degree in it.)

Much of psychology is centered around how our thoughts and emotions affect our behavior, and in turn how we react to new stimuli. My high school percussion instructor drilled this into our heads constantly; the way we talked to ourselves was crucial to how we performed. (Despite doing my best to ignore him, as all teenagers do to adults who are trying to teach them something valuable, I think he might have been right.)

My "thought-to-action pipeline" moment in pickleball happened like this: I was playing singles against my then-fiancé, who had improved faster than me that summer, and I was letting seven or eight points go by without any sign of turning things around, every single game. It was infuriating. It wasn't that I was incapable of doing it, I think my brain was just psyching me out, as brains are wont to do. Then, a little voice in the back of my head pointed out, "He's beatable. He can lose a point. You just have to win this point. That's something can do." I didn't forget about the 2-8 score I was up against, but that reframing was what I needed to win a point and, eventually, catch up. It was almost like *thinking* he was beatable made it possible. The next game, I whispered it aloud to myself, and I ended up beating him in singles for the first time in weeks.

This doesn't mean thinking negatively about your opponents. That won't get you far in such a social sport – or in life. But I also know, especially as a woman, I'm often intimidated, especially if I'm in a new environment and playing with people I don't know. (A lot of pickleball is mixed-gender, too.) I'm also not the most physically fit player, nor am I used to playing team sports. This combination can lead to a lot of doubts, but I urge you to resist them, even if it means literally "gaslighting" yourself a little bit. Next time, think or even say to yourself what you want to be true; that your opponent isn't unbeatable, that you *can* win the next point. It sounds almost too easy, but I've found that it works: Your thoughts can and will change your actions, and that can make all the difference.

So, yeah, as a beginner, you're going to encounter a lot of negative talk – from yourself. And you might not be the most experienced or in-shape or confident. But remember, the way you talk to yourself might help close the gap between you and your goals. From what I've seen, it can make all the difference.

Sub-Lesson 2: Give it Time

If you think that lesson was simple, this one is even simpler. In a world where we're accustomed to everything happening immediately, patience can be really hard. But although I'm only 24, I've noticed something about time that might help you approach pickleball. (And what do you know? Life as well!)

My dad talks extensively about letting go of your anger and learning to turn it into something more constructive. It's amazing to have a role model like that; he is always trying to step out of his comfort zone to get better, which often means looking inward and calming the buzzing brain. I'm trying to do that, too, but I also share his frustrations over a bad shot or bad game. I'm a decidedly sore loser at times, especially when it comes to silly mistakes.

When I first started playing, it was only with Chase or Dad; I was way too intimidated to ask anyone else. Walk up to another person, a stranger, and *talk* to them? But that meant I was always playing with people better than me. So, I lost a lot. I remember being very discouraged at first; maybe this sport isn't for me? But I kept going, mostly because I really needed the exercise, and luckily having my partner with me made it so much easier. Then, eventually, I hit some good shots. *Some of them were even on purpose!* It was an incredible feeling to have my dad, my role model in pickleball and life, give me a "nice shot!" Months later, I've noticed that when I inevitably flub a backhand or drop an easy shot into the net, it stings a little less.

The lesson: You need to give new things time so you can start to average the ups and downs. Beginnings have so many more downs, it can feel like a huge loss, but if you can forge ahead anyway, that net score balances out. I promise it's worth it, whether it's pickleball, crocheting, or baking. Give yourself a chance to feel both the ups and downs first, and then you can have a better perspective on your experience and continue from there. Like I said, it could make all the difference.

YOU WIN SOME, YOU LEARN SOME

I don't recall where I first heard this phrase – magazine article, I think – but it immediately took root in my brain.

I'm highly competitive; I hate to lose. And I never found much solace in the original version of that saying: You win some, you *lose* some. "Yeah, but losing sucks," I'd think.

It sounds almost ridiculously simple, reframing it this way, but it's genius: Every loss is an opportunity to learn something. What did I learn when I came up short in my second singles tournament? That I needed to work on my endurance; I'd been gassed after the very first game. What did I learn after getting crushed by those 80-something Floridians? That you don't judge a book by its cover.

Instead of sitting around and moping over the loss, I have the opportunity to "review the game tape," so to speak, to ask what I might have done differently for a better outcome and how I can improve for the next match.

I've also realized (and this is an offshoot of what I discussed in Lesson 11) that you can learn "in the moment," not just after the fact. Earlier

I told you about ladder leagues, where you have the chance to move up (or down) a court from one week to the next, depending on your performance. Back in the spring of this year I joined a six-week league at The Hawk in Farmington Hills, Michigan – but had to miss the first week due to travel. That meant instead of getting placed based on my performance (as noted earlier, the first week is the "sorting hat"), I'd go into week two with a zero score – and that meant starting on court five. The lowest court, with the lowest-scoring players. If I wanted any shot at winning the league, I'd need to claw my way up to court one, then score the most points there in that final week.

Impossible. For starters, there were lots of great players standing between me and court one. Along the way, for example, I played against Scott, an amazing net-defender; Steve, with a cannon of a forehand and a perpetual smile on his face; and, eventually, my old Sports Club buddy Marty, whose game has improved in parallel with mine these past couple years and who'd already made it to court one.

I often feel a strong sense of Imposter Syndrome when I play in leagues and tournaments; I watch others on the court and think, "Wow, they're good. No way can I beat those guys." (Yeah, I'm still grappling with decades' worth of negativity and self-doubt. It'll probably take more than a couple years of modest pickleball success to unravel it.)

Nevertheless, week by week, I won my round, and in the final session I found myself standing on court one. It's funny how you can argue with yourself: I believe I'm fairly troll-like in appearance, yet my wife is stunningly beautiful and so I can't understand why she picked me. I battled my way to the top court, yet I think there must be some mistake; I'm not a good enough player to be there.

Stupid brain.

Having scouted that court in the weeks prior, I knew there were two guys – Joe and Brennan – who were largely unbeaten. If I'm a 4.0 player, they're probably 4.5 or higher. Spoiler alert: This doesn't end with me winning the league or even winning my games against Joe and Brennan; I lost both of them.

But rather than lick my wounds on the sidelines after those losses, I did something different: I decided to watch their remaining games, to see if I could determine what tools they had in their skillset that I lacked. How did they return serves so effectively? When did they slice a forehand instead of smashing it? And why did some opponents have no trouble returning that slice while others (myself included) sent it into the net?

In other words, if I couldn't win against them, what could I *learn* from them? This mindset was like a refreshing drink on a hot day, and it came on the heels of a lifetime's worth of scorchers. When I sat reflecting on this later, I recognized countless times I should have looked for the lesson instead of dwelling on the defeat.

There's a scene in an episode of *The Simpsons*, "Mom and Pop Art," that has always resonated with me. Homer attempts to build a backyard barbecue pit, and of course the results are disastrous. First we see the picture on the box, then the hilariously mangled final product – followed by Homer's anguished cry: "WHY?! Why… must… life… be so hard!? Why must I fail at every attempt at masonry!?"

I feel you, brother.

But isn't the goal to do better next time? Not just in pickleball, but in life? I'm undoubtedly thicker-headed than most, as it took 55 years and a whiffle-ball to learn that, but I'm glad I got here eventually. I'll do better in my next life.

Nelson Mandela said it best:

> *I never lose. I either win or learn.*

LAST LOBS

Teamwork and communication. Adaptability and flexibility. Persistence, patience, resilience, sportsmanship. These are some of the words an AI bot coughed up when I asked it what lessons pickleball could teach us. And this is why I'll likely be out of a job before long, because it pretty much nailed it. (Luckily, I can be broke and still play. Compared with most other sports, this one is *cheap*.)

I suppose those things apply to lots of other games as well, but nothing else I've played – or done – in my life brought them to the fore the way pickleball has.

But you forgot something, 'bot, and I almost did, too: Joy.

During the Pandemic, I felt the same hopelessness and despair as pretty much everyone on the planet. All the self-help gurus preached about "finding joy," looking for the things that made you happy. I tried and came up empty. Wake up, sit at the keyboard all day, go to bed. Wash, rinse, repeat. The few hobbies I had – kickboxing, going to the movies, even trying new restaurants – were gone, closed off, unavailable.

Where was the joy in my life? In absentia.

When I play pickleball, I feel joyous. And not just because the game is fun and gets the heart rate up, but because of the people. I'm surround by smiles and laughter, camaraderie and bonhomie… what is that if not joy?

It's enough to make you want to write a book about it.

And I'll admit, the hardest part about that was taking time away from pickleball. (The best part about it was allowing myself use of the Oxford comma, which my workplace forbids.) But if you learned a little about the game, and perhaps even yourself, I'll consider the time very well spent.

There were lots of other anecdotes I wanted to share and people I wanted to mention, but for various reasons they didn't find a home in the previous chapters. A few notables:

🏓 While nothing beats the experience of taking lessons and playing as much as possible, you can learn a lot from YouTube. It's home to countless videos on understanding the basics, improving your serve, mastering third-shot drops, and much more. When I'm not playing pickleball, I'm watching videos about pickleball. (And don't miss the parodies! Start with "The 5 Stages of Pickleball" and "The Pickleball Song," both by The Holderness Family.)

🏓 I'll never forget the brassy 70-something Florida woman who'd hit a winner and then crow to the other team, "Any questions?"

(Same woman to her partner a few minutes later, after he'd missed an easy ball: "Nice shot, Stevie… Wonder.")

🏓 Ernie, muttering after other Rick's unforced error: "He can't dink *or* drive."

🏓 My daughter, new to the game but already developing into a superb player, describes herself as "the Lob-ster" – someone who expertly lofts the ball overhead and into a far corner. And I'm overjoyed that she and her husband, Chase, play together. Pickleball is without question the world's best couples' sport.

● After contorting my body to get out of the way of a ball hit directly at me, my partner Steve said, "Nice Matrix." (I looked like Keanu Reeves' Neo dodging slow-motion bullets.)

● Mike, who works at Pickle Rage of West Bloomfield, and who I met just as I was wrapping up the book, bellowed this after hitting a ball that soared miles past the baseline: "In or out?" (The accompanying huge smile helped land the joke.)

● "Pickleball amnesia" is very real. It's when four people collectively forget who just served and what the score is. There is no known cure.

● There's some great pickleball merch out there, especially shirts. Some of my favorites:

- I dink, therefore I am
- I can't, I have pickleball
- Ask me about my dinking problem
- I like pickleball and maybe three people
- Whose Serve? What's the Score? What Day is It? Who Are You People?

Now, if you'll excuse me, I'm needed on the court. Wanted, even. Imagine that.

EPILOGUE

September 15, 2024

I often wonder how a painter knows when the painting is done. Was *that* the last brushstroke? Does it need one more? When does it become too many?

For an author, there's a similar struggle – though at least I always have the option of removing strokes if they're uglying up the thing. When is it time to call it a day? I don't like to overstay my welcome, but I also don't want to leave money on the table.

About two weeks ago, I decided the book was done. I'd learned all the possible lessons and set them in type as best I could. To the printing press! Let's get this thing published already.

Self-published, to be accurate, but the service I'd enlisted for that purpose left me stymied. So much information needed, so many cryptic forms to complete. Documents to be formatted, uploaded, reformatted. I obtained the necessary ISBN numbers, only to find that those required information and forms of their own. And in the interim, I was back and forth almost daily with the cover-art designer.

In other words, you don't just type "The End", press a button, then wait for Oprah's people to call. It takes a lot to publish a book, and I kept dead-ending in the maze.

Of course, wrong turns often yield serendipitous results. Go left instead of right and you might find yourself standing before the best donut shop on the planet. Had I published sooner, I'd have missed getting smacked in the head with one of the biggest lessons of all.

It happened only yesterday, during a four-hour pickleball clinic – my first real instruction since Traci Bruletti's "Patience-ball" session.

The instructor, who I'll call Sean (owing to his passing resemblance to actor Sean Hayes), had arranged for our small group to meet at the country home of "Rusty" (the nickname I've bestowed based on his hair color). Rusty had built two world-class courts in his backyard, and was graciously hosting the clinic – as well as participating in it.

As I navigated to Rusty's address, my route led me out of the suburbs, along quiet two-lane roads that eventually gave way to a narrow dirt road. Along the way, I spotted a growing number of political signs – this was about six weeks before the 2024 election – and felt greater unease with each one I passed.

Let's just say, the signs were not for my preferred candidate.

Everybody relax, I'm not about to "go political." I'm about to "go pickleball."

But the context must come first: This year has been a real struggle, even more so than the ones preceding the previous two elections. More than ever, I grapple to understand how voters on the other side can possibly stay on that side, even while recognizing that those voters feel the same about me and my side. We are, all of us, uncomprehending.

This division has caused some fraying in relationships with friends and family members. All of it seems so big, so all-encompassing, it threatens to swallow everything else. How can we be so far apart on this? And because we are, are we enemies now?

Like I said: a struggle. So every time I see one of those yard signs, I'm reminded of the division, the animosity, the polishing of philosophical bayonets.

The last thing I wanted was for any of this to spill into today's session. And as I pulled into Rusty's driveway, I breathed a sigh of relief: no signs in the yard. Cool, let's get some sunscreen on and start mastering the third-shot drop.

I walked around back, shook hands with Sean, admired the incredible courts (Oh, to have these in my own backyard!). Then I turned to greet Rusty. Older gent, probably mid-70s, muscular and impressively hale for his age. At that point I'd yet to nickname him because I couldn't see his hair; he was wearing a hat. A political hat. A very, very political hat.

It felt like a kick in the gut. Day ruined, I thought, or at least tarnished. I have to spend four hours staring at this brazen reminder of all this turmoil? I mean, Rusty's house, Rusty's rules; he can wear what he likes, obviously. But as I mentioned early on, pickleball is (almost) always my safe-space. This felt like such an intrusion. A provocation. An insult, even.

Once everyone else arrived, Sean introduced himself, sharing his pickleball origin story, his plans for the day, and his philosophy about the game. He spoke eloquently about its ability to create community and "how important that is right now." (Aha, I thought, an ally, perhaps?)

Then we got to Rusty, who proved more reticent than I'd expected; he talked a bit about his work background (retired metal-worker) and not much else. To my relief, he said nothing about his hat or anything related to it. In fact, he surprised me by extolling the virtues of bringing together "like-minded people." He couldn't have meant politically like-minded, because he couldn't know where any of us stood. He must have meant pickleball-minded! What else could it be?

I started wondering which of us had the chip on his shoulder.

The day unfolded exactly as I hoped it would. Sean imparted some useful lessons; we did drills and played little games that had everyone scrambling and laughing. Occasionally I found myself on the same side of the net as Rusty, who shared my penchant for mumbling at himself after a bad shot. He also complimented me on my serve; I told him I admired his quick reach at the net.

During these long months of fretting over the ugly political scene, I've tried to remember a few simple (if clichéd) truths:

- There's more that unites us than divides us
- People have reasons for believing what they believe and voting the way they do
- The nature of our political system is that it necessarily pits us against each other. But I don't want to be pitted against others, especially people I care about!

There, on the pickleball court, we were all just pickleball players, trying to improve our game and, as always, have fun.

Rusty wasn't my enemy, any more than I was his. We simply had different opinions about this one thing. Not an unimportant thing, but also not the defining thing.

If only politics worked like pickleball. Two teams, respectful of their opponents, strategic, thoughtful, playing to win but playing fair. Celebrating victories but respecting defeats. Meeting at the net when it's all over. Paddle-tap. Good game. Wanna go again?

The world I want to live in is the world I encounter on the pickleball court. Let's have fun together. Let's compliment each other when we do well and work to improve when we don't. Let's run and laugh and burn some calories. Then do it all again tomorrow, because we like being together.

Maybe we should call it Peace-ball.

ACKNOWLEDGEMENTS

It was all me.

That's a joke, one I stole from Allison Janney's acceptance speech for her 2018 Oscar. Obviously she had help getting to the podium, just as I had help getting these pages into your hands.

Needless to say, I couldn't have done it without the endless support, encouragement, and enthusiasm of my amazing wife of 30 years. If everyone had a Shawna in their lives, the world would be a happier place.

Right around the time I hatched the idea for this book, Shawna and I had dinner with some new friends, Pam and Garry Cole. Garry was writing his own book, "Are We Old Yet?", with plans to self-publish. Any doubts I had about whether to start my own project were erased by Garry's enthusiasm and perseverance. He wasn't a writer, had no experience with publishing, yet he powered through and made it happen. (With great results, by the way – his book combines entertaining personal stories with extensive research on aging. Highly recommended.)

Garry not only provided the template for what I'd need to do, but also the assurance that, yes, I could do it. For a non-pickleball player, he's an awfully good guy – and I'm grateful to have him as a friend.

Thanks as well to everyone who took the time to read my drafts: Dave, Caroline, Bill, Mom, Sarah, Chase, and especially Wendy (she of "no sorrys in pickleball" fame). Beyond our court interactions, I didn't know

Wendy very well, but my gut told me she was someone worth knowing – and someone who could help me make the book better. After a single meeting over coffee, I learned I was right on both counts.

Thanks to Dr. Jason Novetsky for giving some random guy off the street a generous helping of his time and insight.

Thanks to life coach Ryan Burtanog for lending his expertise as well.

And thanks, finally, to the amazing people I've met on this journey, including (but in no way limited to): Marty and Tracy, Dan and Tracy, Jay and Sheree. Sherrie, Amy, Jodi, Barry, Nancy. Lauren, Trudy, Ganesh. Keith. Steve C. Sue and Beth. Jim M., Scott, Rick, Ernie.

Your smiles, kind words, openness, and encouragement have made me a happier person. I'll do my best to repay that by paying it forward to others I meet.

And speaking of meeting… what time tomorrow?